LIFTOFF!

DATE DUE

SILVER BURDETT PRESS
Parsippany, New Jersey

To mom and dad, who gave me wings to fly.

© 1995 by R. Mike Mullane

Illustrations ©1995 by Mike Wimmer

Published by Silver Burdett Press,
A Paramount Communications Company
299 Jefferson Road, Parsippany, NJ 07054

Designed by Marie Fitzgerald

Manufactured in Mexico

10 9 8 7 6 5 4 3 2 1

Library of Congress Cataloging-in-Publication Data
Mullane, R. Mike.
Liftoff!: an astronaut's dream / by R. Mike Mullane;
illustrated by Mike Wimmer. p. cm.
1. Space flight—Juvenile literature. 2. Atlantis (Space
shuttle)—Juvenile literature. 3. Mullane, R. Mike.
4. Astronauts—United States—Biography. [1. Space
flight. 2. Astronautics. 3. Mullane, R. Mike.
4. Astronauts.] I. Wimmer, Mike, ill. II. Title.
TL793.M79 1995 629.45′4—dc20
94-18122 CIP AC

ISBN 0-382-24663-2

ISBN 0-382-24664-0 (pbk.)

"*Atlantis*, the weather plane is making one last check of some clouds, and as soon as the pilot gives us a clearance, we'll continue the countdown."

The commander answers the launch director's call. "Roger. We're ready."

I hear the announcement through my "Snoopy" cap head-set and think, *Please, let the weather be okay and let us launch.*

I'm mission specialist 1, seated right behind the pilot, in the cockpit of the space shuttle *Atlantis*. I'm ready for my second ride into space. I'm also miserable. I wiggle in my seat to try to get comfortable, but it's impossible. I have eighty-five pounds of equipment wrapped around my body: long underwear, pressure suit, boots, helmet, gloves, para-chute, oxygen bottles, life raft, and survival harness. There are straps coming over my shoulders, between my legs, and around my waist, all holding me tightly to the steel chair. The space shuttle seats are not couches like the ones they had in the old days of the space program. Then, there were just a few astronauts. Now, there are many, and it would be too expensive to build separate couches for all their different sizes. So the seats are all the same, just flat plates of heavy steel with thin cushions covering them. They're torture to lie in and I've been lying in mine for the past four hours waiting for the weather to clear. Try tilting your chair on the floor and then lying in it for a couple of hours on your back. You'll have a sense of what an astronaut feels like waiting for launch.

And the diaper I'm wearing is soaked. Yes! A diaper! Astronauts wear diapers during launch. When you're in a spacesuit and strapped on your back to a seat, you can't get up and use the shuttle toilet. A diaper is the only solution. Actually, there are three times when an astronaut has to wear a diaper: during launch, during reentry, and during a space walk. During each of those times, it's impossible to get to the toilet. So, I'm lying in a very wet diaper, knowing why babies cry when they have wet diapers. It's gross!

I try to gain some relief from the pain by inflating my pressure suit. It expands like a big, orange balloon and gives me a little room to wiggle. Actually, it *is* a balloon. It's a balloon in the shape of a suit. We wear them during launch and reentry in case a window should break or air should leak out of the cockpit for any reason. If that ever happened, and we weren't wearing pressure suits, our blood would boil inside our skin and we would die. The suit has nothing to do with the g-force pressure of the rocket

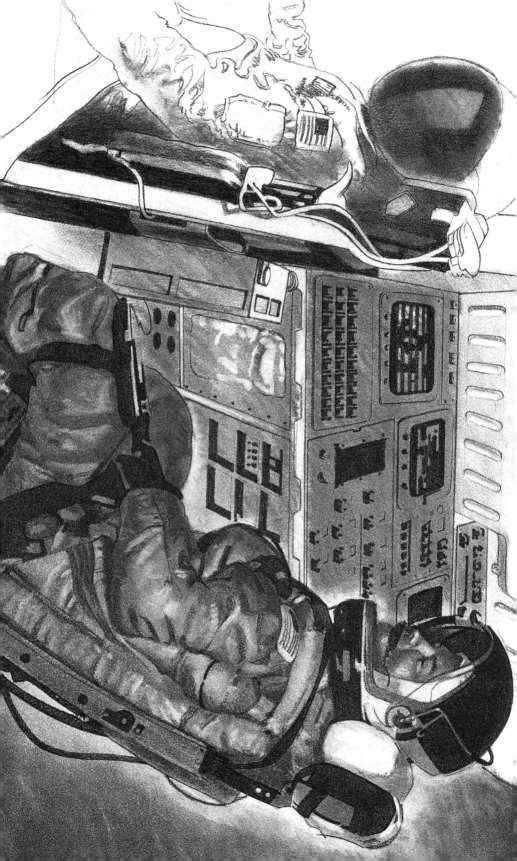

pushing us. Rather, the word *pressure* refers to the need to keep air pressure on our skin so our blood doesn't boil.

"*Atlantis*, the weather pilot just reported that the clouds are no longer a problem. We'll be coming out of the hold in five seconds . . . four . . . three . . . two . . . one . . . T-minus nine minutes and counting."

"Roger, we see the clock running."

I silently shout for joy, *Finally, we're counting down to launch!* Each of the three computer screens has a digital countdown clock flickering toward zero.

Humming, whirring, flashing electronic boxes are now checking everything about the shuttle and sending the information, the *data*, to the Mission Control team. The thought of that wonderful team of men and women watching over us erases a little of the fear that we feel.

Astronauts get the "glory" part of a space mission. You see them floating around the cockpit and doing space walks. You see their pictures in the newspapers and the president shaking their hands. But have you ever thought about the rest of the NASA team? It takes thousands of people working together as a team to accomplish a space mission. Nobody can do it alone. It's just like a football or soccer team. The person who scores the winning goal is the one who gets the cheers. But did he or she win the game alone? No. Somebody else passed the ball. Somebody else blocked. Nobody wins the game and nobody flies into space without a lot of help. It's a team effort. Everybody depends on everybody else.

"Okay, review your emergency escape procedures."

The order is from the commander. He wants us to look over the procedures we would have to follow in case there is an emergency before launch. Remember, we are sitting on top of four million pounds of dangerous fuel. If something went wrong and there was a fire before liftoff, we would want to shut off the engines and get away as quickly as possible.

I look at the checklist of emergency procedures that is stuck with Velcro on the back of the pilot's seat. It tells me the steps I would need to follow to release my seat belts, oxygen hoses, and communications cords. Then, it says I should crawl from the cockpit, run across the launch pad platform (called the *gantry*), and jump into a basket hanging two hundred feet above the ground. As I read the steps, I think, *I hope I never have to do this!* It would be an awesome ride, like something out of an Indiana Jones movie, but it would also be very scary.

Just imagine for a moment that it's happening to you. . . .

"*Atlantis!* We see a fuel leak! Get out! Mode 1 egress! Mode 1 egress!" *Egress* means "exit." The launch team has detected an emergency that might cause the shuttle to explode, and they want you to escape using the basket.

Because you've just reviewed your emergency procedures, it takes you only a moment to release all the connections that hold you to the seat. Next, you roll off your seat and crash onto the back instrument panel. Remember, the shuttle is standing on its tail, so the back wall of the cockpit is the "floor."

There's no room to stand, so you crawl to the side hatch.

In ten seconds you have it open and crawl out onto the gantry. Water is everywhere! What's going on? Then you remember. The launch team has turned on the water sprinklers to help protect you from any fire.

After making certain that the rest of the crew is out of the shuttle, you run through the water spray and jump into an escape basket. The ground is two hundred feet straight down and the basket swings and bounces. You think, *This is the scariest thing I've ever done.*

BAM! You smash your fist onto a paddle that cuts a cord and releases the basket. This begins your escape from the launch pad. You can't go down the stairs or the elevator. It would take too long. Besides, if there were a fire at the bottom of the gantry, running down the stairs or taking an elevator would put you right in the middle of it. The escape basket takes you to the ground while moving you *away* from the rocket. It slides on a steel cable that stretches sideways a thousand feet from the launch pad.

What a ride! A loud hiss comes from the cable as the basket accelerates. The ground rushes toward you. If you crash into it, you'll be killed. What's going to stop you?

WHAM! Just before the basket reaches the ground, it slaps into a net hung between two poles. The net drags your basket to a stop.

But you're still not safe. Even though you're a thousand feet from the launch pad, a big explosion could kill you. Get going!

You jump from the basket and run into a nearby underground bunker. Or maybe you decide the danger is so great that even the bunker wouldn't protect you. So you get in an old Armored Personnel Carrier (called an APC for short, it looks something like a tank), and drive away. NASA parks an APC near the bunker for that purpose.

Good job! It took you only four minutes and thirty-five seconds to unstrap from your seat, get out of the shuttle, run to the basket, and slide down the cable.

My countdown continues. The clock shows T-minus six minutes.

I check that all of my straps are tight. There will be a lot of vibration during launch. I double-check that my parachute is attached. After the solid-fueled boosters burn out and the liquid-fueled engines stop, the space shuttle is a glider. In a launch emergency, there's always the possibility that we might not be able to glide to a runway for landing. In that case we would bail out, using the parachutes attached to our backs. After floating into the ocean, we would get in small life rafts that are also folded up and clipped to our backs. We hope we could stay alive long enough for a helicopter to reach us.

"*Atlantis*, start the APUs."

The call comes from the launch director. The countdown has reached T-minus five minutes, and it's time to start the hydraulic motors that will steer the three giant rocket engines. APUs stands for Auxiliary Power Units. Calling every piece of equipment by its complete name would be tongue twisting, so astronauts and the rest of the NASA team use abbreviations like APU, IMU, EPS, MPS, MECO, and MLS. We learn hundreds of them during our training.

9

The APU switches are on the pilot's side, so I watch him follow the checklist. Everything an astronaut does is written on a checklist. The walls, ceiling, and instrument panel are papered with them. Why do we use checklists? You never see anybody on *Star Trek* using a checklist. But *Star Trek* is make-believe. Nobody on Captain Picard's *Enterprise* is really going to die if he or she makes a mistake. But in the real world, a mistake could threaten an astronaut's life. There are nearly two thousand switches and controls in the shuttle cockpit, so a mistake is certainly possible. Even though we practice the mission until we know what every one of those switches does, we never trust our memories. We always do things by following our checklists.

The APU motors are at the back of the shuttle, but as they start I can feel their vibrations in the cockpit. For the first time, I get the sensation that the machine is alive. It's like some giant beast stirring from its sleep.

No longer do I think about my backache and wet diaper. Now, I'm scared. In just a few minutes *Atlantis* will lift off in a thunderous cloud of fire and smoke. With such enormous power, there is a lot that can go wrong and put us in danger. The rocket has many parts. It's a very complicated machine. So, in these last few minutes before launch, I'm scared. My heart pounds inside my chest. I can feel it in my throat . . . THUD . . . THUD . . . THUD . . . like I've just run a race. I try to swallow, but my mouth is dry. Fear does that to you. It makes your heart pound and your mouth feel like it's full of cotton.

"*Atlantis*, close visors."

"Roger. Closing visors."

The countdown has reached T-minus two minutes, and the checklist says to close our helmet visors. These are the clear plastic coverings on the faces of the helmets. Before I close mine, I pull a drink container from a Velcro patch on the wall and suck down a few swallows of water through a plastic straw. The container has the same design as the ones we use during orbit, a foil pouch with a straw at the end. I clip the straw closed, reattach the container to the Velcro, and lock my visor down. A cool flow of oxygen swirls around my face. If a window should break during launch, now I'm completely protected.

The beast awakens some more. I can feel it shaking. The computers are making a final check of the steering controls, causing the rocket to sway back and forth. The bottoms of the two solid-fueled rocket motors are held to the launch pad by eight giant threaded nuts, so I know we can't fall over. Still, the shaking is another indication that the shuttle is readying itself to fly. My fear increases and my breathing becomes faster. I can hear it inside the sealed helmet . . . SSSSSSSSSS . . . SSSSSSSSSS . . . SSSSSSSSSS . . . as air is inhaled and exhaled.

The movies always make it look like astronauts are never afraid. But that's not true. We know flying into space is dangerous and there's a chance we could be killed. So we're scared. At the same time, though, our hearts are ready to explode with happiness. Many of us have dreamed all our lives of flying into space. Now, that dream is about to come true, so we're joyous. In a small way, getting on a roller coaster gives you the same feeling. You're afraid, but you're happy, too.

"One minute."

The instruments begin to change as the engine system prepares to start. Green, glowing digits on the computers flicker with new data. Meters move. The beast is more alive than ever, and my heart pounds deeper and faster.

I think of my family, of my wife and my three teenage children. They are three miles away on the roof of the LCC, the Launch Control Center. I know they are more scared than any of us inside the rocket. It may be *Atlantis* standing on the launch pad, but in their minds they can only see *Challenger*. That was the space shuttle that blew up in 1986 and killed its crew. I know my family fears the same thing will happen to me.

It's always much harder to watch somebody you love do something dangerous than it is to be the one in danger. Can you remember when you were learning to ride a bike? I'll bet you were very scared the first time you wobbled along without training wheels. But I know your parents were more scared because they were afraid you would get hurt. In this final minute before the engines start, I know it's that way with my wife and children. I know they are clutching each other and praying for my safety. I love them even more for their courage to stand on that roof and watch *Atlantis* take me to my dream.

"T-minus ten seconds. Go for main engine start."

Atlantis's computers are ready to start the engines.

There's nothing to do now but watch the instruments. Astronauts don't really fly the shuttle into orbit. Things happen too fast for an astronaut to control, so we have to depend on the computers. We watch the instruments while they steer us into orbit. Only if something went terribly wrong would we try to fly the shuttle the way a pilot flies an airplane.

"T-minus nine . . . eight . . ."

"Seven . . . six . . . main engine start."

The three liquid-fueled engines ignite, and there is a deafening noise in the cockpit. A growling, wrenching vibration shakes us. I have to force myself to keep watching the instruments. It's like trying to read a book on a theme park ride. The noise and vibration and the thrill and fear make it impossible to concentrate.

"Five . . . four . . . three . . . "

The countdown continues while *Atlantis's* computers check that the liquid-fueled engines are working okay. The three liquid-fueled engines are started early because they can be turned off if something is wrong, just as a car engine can be turned off. But the solid-fueled boosters on the sides of the shuttle are like bottle rockets on the Fourth of July. Once they're started, they cannot be turned off. Only at the very last moment, when the countdown reaches zero, will they be ignited.

"Two . . . one . . . liftoff!"

The solid-fueled rocket boosters ignite, the threaded nuts holding them to the pad explode into pieces, and the giant machine blasts from the launch pad. The noise is incredible! Only because I'm wearing a helmet can I hear Mission Control talking to us. The engines are so powerful that I'm shoved backwards into my seat by a force one-and-a-half times as strong as gravity. It makes my body and everything I'm wearing seem to weigh an extra hundred pounds.

"Roll program!" the commander shouts into his microphone. *Atlantis* is rolling to the right to aim its trajectory over the ocean.

"Throttle down!" The commander sees that our engines are automatically reducing power. *Atlantis* is accelerating too fast and there is a danger that the thick atmosphere will tear it apart. The computers prevent this from happening by commanding the engines to pull back their power.

Shock waves form on the nose and wings and add to the shaking. *Atlantis* is going through the sound barrier. In just forty seconds the huge engines and solid-fueled rocket boosters have pushed a four-and-a-half-*million*-pound machine straight up to the speed of sound! Just imagine the incredible power needed to do that. The rushing sound of supersonic air howls around the machine. It's louder than any airplane you've ever heard. The vibrations increase. My eyes skip from instrument to instrument. Is everything still okay? Will all this shaking damage something? Will our air leak out? Will the engines quit? Will they explode? I

worry about everything. But the instruments tell me that *Atlantis* is *nominal*, that everything is okay.

A cloud zooms into our windshield and disappears behind us. Once again, I can feel my body being squeezed backwards. It's happening because the engines are returning to full power. We're above the thick atmosphere and don't have to worry anymore about the air pressure tearing *Atlantis* apart. The ride is smoothing out.

There is no line that you pass where all the air is below and space is above. The atmosphere just keeps getting thinner and thinner, and as it does, the sky changes from blue to black. It becomes as black as night. Sirius, the brightest star, appears. It's so strange to see a black sky and a bright star while sunlight is filling the cockpit, but that's what I see from the shuttle windows.

"PC less than fifty!" The numbers are flashing on our computer, and the commander calls them to Mission Control. The pressure inside the solid-fueled rocket motors has decreased to fifty pounds per square inch. That means the boosters are nearly out of fuel.

BANG! WHOOSH!

A loud bang shakes the cockpit, and a flash of yellow fire covers the windshield.

Has something exploded? Is there an emergency?

No. The noise and fire are from the release of the giant boosters. They have burned out, and small rockets on their noses and tails have blown them away from the shuttle. Parachutes will lower them into the ocean where tugboats will pick them up so they can be used over again.

As the boosters fall away, total silence comes to the cockpit. It's a silence as empty as the sky in our windows. We are so high now that the air is too thin for sound to be able to travel. We can't hear any noise from our three liquid-fueled engines or hear any air rushing by the cockpit. The ride becomes as smooth as glass. The only feeling we have of being thrust into space is an increasing force on our bodies. As the engines draw the liquid fuel out of the big orange belly tank and burn it, the rocket gets lighter and lighter. It goes faster and faster, and we get squeezed backwards into our seats. Imagine being in a dark, quiet room with an invisible hand pushing on your chest. That's what it feels like.

"*Atlantis,* you're two-engine TAL."

"Roger, Houston."

The call from Mission Control means that we are now high enough and going fast enough that if one of our engines quits, we could fly across the Atlantic Ocean and make an emergency landing in Europe. If that happened, it would be a thirty-five-minute flight. It takes an airplane seven hours, but in a space shuttle you fly across the ocean in just thirty-five minutes!

"*Atlantis,* you're negative return."

"Roger, Houston. Negative return."

We always repeat to Mission Control what they tell us, so they know we've heard them correctly. This latest call, "negative return," means that we're now too far away and going too fast to be able to make an emergency landing back at the Kennedy Space Center. Now, if anything goes wrong and we can't reach orbit, we have to fly straight ahead to an emergency field in Africa or Europe.

One of the crew members is a rookie, and he lets out a cheer. It seems strange, doesn't it, that an astronaut would cheer while this dangerous ride is still going on? But he has good reason to celebrate. *Atlantis* has just passed fifty miles altitude. What's so special about that? The official definition of an astronaut is anybody who has traveled at least fifty miles above the earth. The man cheering is a rookie, so this is the first time he's ever gotten high enough to be an "official" astronaut.

"*Atlantis,* you're press to MECO."

"Roger, Houston. Press to MECO."

Now the space shuttle is going so fast and is so high that if one of its engines quits, we could still make it to MECO, Main Engine Cut-Off. We could limp into orbit on two engines.

Higher! Higher and faster! The velocity meter shows our incredible speeds . . . thirteen . . . fifteen . . . seventeen . . . twenty times the speed of sound!

Atlantis is leveling its nose, silently tearing into the black of space. Throughout the entire flight, it slowly has gone from pointing straight up to being nearly level with the earth.

Twenty-one . . . twenty-two . . . twenty-three times the speed of sound!

My heart is thumping wildly. But it's not from fear. Now, it's from the thrill of the adventure. Once again, I'm going into space! Once again, the joy of having a dream come true is sweeping over me! I want to scream my happiness! I want to shout for all the world to hear! I'm going into space! I'm an astronaut!

I can still see myself as a small child, dreaming about flying. It was almost as if I was born with that dream. Perhaps it was the influence of my father, who had flown on bombers during World War II and who was flying on Air Force transport planes as I was growing up. He often took my brothers and sister and me to see airplanes. He would take us into the cockpit and let us sit in the pilot's seat and touch the controls. I would grab the steering wheel (it's called the *yoke*) and for a few moments pretend I was flying. Was it this early fun with airplanes that gave me the dream of flight? Of course I can never know for sure, but in my dimmest, most distant memories, my dream was to fly. I was in love with the sky and everything in it.

Before I could read, I drew pictures of swirling, diving airplanes with dashed pencil lines coming from their noses and wings. The dashes were the machine-gun fire. In my imagination, I was in the cockpit of that fighter, shooting an enemy plane from the sky. My childhood was a time when there was great fear in the world. World War II had ended, but the Cold War had replaced it. Everybody was afraid that Russian bombers would drop atomic bombs on American cities. In school we practiced air raid drills and hid under our desks. I imagined that someday I would be in a fighter jet and would shoot down Russian bombers. I thought it would be fun to be in combat. Many years later, in the skies over Vietnam, I would learn a much different reality.

But as a child, when I went to bed on Christmas Eve, the only reality was toys. I prayed that Santa would bring me models of the fastest jet fighter planes. Even their names made my imagination fly at light speed: *Starfighter, Super Sabre, Shooting Star, Thunder Chief, Delta Dagger.*

For my birthdays, I wanted balsa wood gliders and airplane coloring books. I made Tinker-Toy airplanes and Erector-Set airplanes and paper airplanes and would run around the house holding them in my hand and making roaring sounds like a dive bomber. I used cloth and thread from my mother's sewing cabinet to make parachutes for my little plastic pilots.

As I grew older, my interest in flying and the sky intensified. I began to design my own gliders powered by rubber bands. Some flew magnificently, soaring silently across the nearby New Mexican desert. I would chase my creation and try to grab it before it ran out of power and crashed into a tumbleweed. Other designs crashed as soon as I released them. Hours of work would end up in a pile of splintered balsa wood and fabric covering. Back in my room, I would make a change and try again. I didn't realize it then, but I was already learning something very important to a scientist and engineer. I was learning how to experiment. I was learning how to ask a question and then design a test to find the answer.

Some experiments were pretty dumb. One day, I decided to make my own parachute by just holding a sheet over my head and jumping off a high pillar on my grandmother's porch. Needless to say, the experiment failed. I ended up with a broken leg. Dumb! Dumb! Dumb! Don't ever do experiments that put your health and life at risk.

School brightened my dream of flight. I didn't like everything about school. I hated tests and homework and counted the days to summer vacation. But there was a lot that I did like about the classroom. I loved learning about the sky. I loved learning about the weather, about the clouds and lightning, why it rained and why the wind blew. I built my own weather station. Paper cups on a twisted piece of coat hanger wire served as an anemometer (a wind speed instrument). To measure humidity I used a hair from my mom's hairbrush. Did you know that human hair grows and shrinks as the humidity changes? I put a thermometer outside and built a rain gauge. I learned to recognize the different types of clouds: cirrus, cumulus, stratus, and nimbus. I would spend hours watching thunderstorms form over the Albuquerque mountains. What magnificent creations of Nature! Their tops would be churned into giant, white cauliflowers by the summer heat. Skirts of purple rain would gather at their base. Jagged, blue-white forks of lightning would crackle through them and send booms of thunder sweeping across the desert. I loved the sound of that thunder. It was the voice of the sky, calling to me.

Weather fascinated me, but astronomy stole my soul. My most vivid grade-school memory is the day I was first told about our solar system. There were other worlds out there! My imagination bubbled like a volcano! What would it be like to be on another planet? What was Venus like? Mars? Could there be other beings out there? I wanted to know everything about the solar system and the rest of the universe. Before the day was out I had memorized the names of all the planets. I took my science book home and read and reread everything in it about astronomy.

I began my astronomy experiments. First, I decided that I would map the universe. I would plot where every star was located. I took a tablet and a pencil and sat in my front yard and put a dot on the tablet to mark each star I could see. When I got inside and looked at my tablet it was just a crazy bunch of dots. It didn't look anything like the real sky.

Then, I tried to build a telescope by taping a magnifying glass to the end of a toilet paper tube. It didn't work. It made everything look farther away and upside down. But the important thing was that I tried. I experimented. I wanted to know.

Some experiments did work. After learning in class that the earth rotates about an axis that points at the North

Star, I wanted to see for myself. I used my dad's camera to make a time exposure of the northern sky at night. The photos showed a bunch of circles. Those were the streaks of starlight the camera had recorded as the earth turned. It was proof! I felt like Galileo!

Other incredible stories of the heavens came from my teacher and my science books. The starlight that I could see was thousands and thousands of years old. I was looking at a time machine. Cave men were hurling rocks at woolly mammoths when some of the starlight reaching my dad's camera had first left its source. Incredible! What would it have been like to have ridden that beam of light? What would it have been like to have streaked through trillions and trillions of miles of black space? Imagine the sights you would have seen! Imagine the swirling galaxies and planets and moons and asteroids you would have passed. I wanted to take that trip! And I did, time and time again in my dream of flight.

What I wanted most for my eleventh Christmas was a telescope. I imagined myself seeing the things in my science book, the cloud of space dust shaped like a horse's head, and remote galaxies glowing like giant pinwheels. With a telescope I would have a machine that could fly me deeper into space.

Every night for two months leading up to Christmas 1956, I grabbed the Sears catalog and dreamed of its riches. In the past it had been the pages of bicycles and BB guns that I had drooled over. But not this year. Now, it was the pages of telescopes. Sleek beauties with white barrels and mahogany tripods captured my eye. I can see them now as if the pages were in front of me. They were awesome time machines fueled by nothing but light.

On Christmas morning, my wish came true. Standing next to the tree was a telescope with my name on it! I didn't want to look at any other presents. For the first time in my life, I wanted Christmas day to end . . . immediately! I wanted the sun to set and the stars to rise. But the earth's rotation seemed to stop. Time crawled. I busied myself by shining the barrel of the scope. It was brand new and didn't have a speck of dirt on it, but I polished and polished until the white was as gleaming as the stars it would reveal.

Finally, the sun disappeared below the western horizon and . . . a STAR! The evening star had come out! In seconds I had focused my telescope on the tiny point of light. It looked like a small half-moon. Then I remembered: The evening star isn't a star at all. It's a planet. It's Venus. I was seeing Venus! I stared at it and let my imagination fly through the lens, out the tube, and into orbit around the planet. What would the thick clouds look like? Would there be breaks in them so you could see the ground? What would Venus's surface look like? Would there be strange plants or other creatures on it?

A half-moon rose above the mountains. I turned my telescope to it and gasped. It wasn't smooth, the way it looks to the naked eye. Now, hundreds of rugged craters and mountains were visible. The peaks cast razor-sharp shadows and seemed close enough to touch. I had seen many science-fiction movies where men and women had

gone to the moon. That night, with my eye to the telescope, it was easy for me to believe somebody, someday would get there. I wanted it to be me.

Other bright "stars" caught my attention, and I discovered Jupiter and its necklace of moons. I could only see the five or six brightest moons, but it was enough to make me think that we earthlings had been cheated. How come we ended up with only one moon? Wouldn't our sky be much more fun with five moons, or ten, or fifteen?

The rings of Saturn sent my heart into a new flutter of excitement. It was just like the picture in my science book, with a tilted halo surrounding a yellowish ball. Another glorious string of moons laced it.

As the night wore on, I swung my telescope to look at star after star, hoping to find one that was really a distant galaxy. Nothing ever looked like a glowing pinwheel. The telescope was too weak to see any detail across those vast distances. Still, I wasn't disappointed. I felt closer to everything I looked at, including those tiny points of light. Were there planets in orbit about those suns? Was there life out there? Was there some alien child standing in his or her front yard looking at our sun through a telescope and wondering the same thing?

After many hours, I finally folded my treasure and put it in its box. Then, with the cold night air biting at my fingers and ears, I stood for a moment and stared at the dome of the heavens. Venus had set. Saturn and Jupiter and the moon would be up for many more hours. Shooting stars streaked to their deaths in glowing trails of white and orange. I watched and I wished. I wished as only an eleven-year-old can wish. I wished I could fly into space.

"*Atlantis,* you're single-engine press to MECO."

The call from Mission Control means that we are now traveling so fast and are so high that even if two of our engines failed, we could still make it into orbit on the last engine.

We're upside down and, for the first time, Earth appears in our windows. It's an ocean-blue world sprinkled with dazzling white clouds. A border of black space makes the blue and white colors even more intense. It's more beautiful than anything I have ever seen on Earth. It's more beautiful than desert thunderstorms and new-fallen snow and rainbows and waterfalls and everything else I have ever called beautiful.

But we don't see the earth as a ball. Only the astronauts who traveled to the moon have been far enough away to see planet Earth as a ball. For shuttle astronauts the earth is hugely close, like an enormous blue balloon put right up to your face. From our orbit altitude of about two hundred and seventy miles, we can see that the horizon is curved, but we don't see a complete circle.

We're in the final minute of powered flight. Most of our fuel is gone, and *Atlantis's* acceleration crushes us into our seats. We hit two times the force of gravity. Then two and a half. Then three g's. With all the equipment on my body, I now weigh seven hundred and twenty pounds! The air is being squeezed from my lungs, and I struggle to breathe. Talking is done in short grunts. It reminds me of the times when I was a kid wrestling with my brothers and one of them ended up sitting on my chest. I could hardly breathe, just like now. But the force isn't as bad as you see in the science-fiction movies, where it looks like the astronauts' skin is being peeled off their faces.

"The engines are throttling."

The pilot grunts the observation. Though you would think the space shuttle could withstand anything, it really is a fragile machine. It can't take more than three times the force of gravity, or it would tear itself apart. So the engines automatically begin to reduce their power to keep us at three-g's.

On the computer screen I can see the numbers counting down to engine stop . . . three . . . two . . . one . . . zero! The crushing force on my chest is instantly gone. The engines are off. They have pushed *Atlantis* to twenty-five times the speed of sound, or 17,500 miles per hour!

I'm weightless! My arms float up. My body floats underneath the seat belt. Tethered checklists float on the ends of cords like snakes rising to a charmer's flute. The drink container that I used earlier has shaken loose during launch, and now it floats in front of my face. I grab it and stick it to the wall. Then, my eye is caught by something moving, and I turn to see the most amazing sight. A mosquito! It must have flown aboard when the hatch was open. It looks hilarious trying to fly in weightlessness. It's upside down and then right-side up and then turning in a loop.

Here we are just ten seconds in orbit, and we already have an emergency. A loose mosquito is definitely an emergency! I laugh to myself. We've trained for hundreds of hours in simulators to be ready for every possible event. We have stacks of checklists and boxes of tools to get us out of any kind of trouble. But we don't have a can of bug spray! I try to whack our stowaway with my hand, but it flies away.

For a moment, the cockpit is very still and quiet. Then . . . BOOM! BOOM! BOOM! *Atlantis* shivers and shakes. The empty fuel tank is jettisoned, and the commander fires the shuttle's small maneuvering rockets to move us away from the giant container. The tank will burn up in the atmosphere like a meteor.

The shuttle itself would follow the same trajectory and end up in the Indian Ocean if we didn't do something. We're not quite in orbit yet. We need just a little more speed. So the commander fires our OMS (Orbital Maneuvering System) engines to make the final push into orbit. For a minute, we are all shoved back into our seats with a small g-force. Then the two OMS engines shut down and weightlessness returns for good. We're in orbit.

I unsnap my seat belt and remember to use my fingers to propel myself. Fingers allow for better control than legs do. Most of the time legs are in the way in space. They were designed for walking, which is impossible in weightlessness. About the only thing we use legs for is to hold ourselves steady when we want to work on something. We have canvas loops taped to the floor. By sliding our feet under these loops we can have both hands free. So legs aren't really important. In fact, someday I'm sure people who have lost the use of their legs from injury or disease will live and work in space like anybody else. There will be no wheelchairs in space.

Our first real problem develops. A crew member pulls a plastic bag from his pocket and vomits. Nobody understands why, but many astronauts get sick in weightlessness. Even astronauts who have never had motion sickness on Earth have gotten sick in space. And others who do suffer motion sickness on Earth have never been sick in space. It's a big mystery. But those who are bothered by the sickness are usually over it in one or two days.

As you might imagine, throwing up in space is messy. But it's also dangerous. If you are sick enough to throw up, you are also sick enough to make a mistake. And if you were doing a space walk, vomiting could even kill you. You wouldn't be able to get the fluid away from your face, and you could choke to death. Or it could plug up the oxygen circulation system, and you could suffocate. That's one reason why NASA never plans a space walk before the third day in orbit. That way astronauts have time to get over any sickness they might have.

For the next several hours everybody follows the checklist to get the shuttle ready for orbit operations. The commander programs the computers. The pilot shuts off the APUs. The mission specialists open the cargo bay doors and turn on the toilet. Finally, we can change our clothes and take off our diapers. Because of the long, long delay before launch, I notice that I have diaper rash!

After going to the bathroom, I float upstairs to check out the shuttle's robot arm. This is a military mission, and my job will be to use the arm to pick up a giant, secret satellite and release it into space. To do this, I will use two hand controls that look like the joysticks on video games. With these, I will be able to "fly" the arm almost like a pilot flies an airplane. I will steer the end of the arm over a spike on the satellite and squeeze a trigger that wraps a cable around the spike. Then, I will be able to lift the satellite up. But that's on tomorrow's checklist. For now, I just use the two joysticks to lift the robot arm from its cradle. Then I float downstairs to help with the experiments.

Many of the experiments are designed to help scientists better understand how the human body adjusts to weightlessness. We check our vision by looking into a box that has an eye test. We chew on cotton balls and put them in test tubes so that doctors can later analyze our saliva. We take measurements of our calves and thighs and find that we have lost several inches. It isn't because we have lost weight, though. It's because the extra body fluid that used to be held in our legs by gravity is now equally spread through our bodies. Our legs have gotten skinnier, but our chests and faces have gotten fatter. That's where the fluid has gone.

We also measure our height. Would you believe that we are almost two inches taller than we were on Earth? What's happening? The reason we've grown taller is that the vertebrae in our spines are no longer crunched together by gravity. They have spread apart, lengthened our spines, and made us taller.

Another experiment involves testing how much space radiation astronauts are exposed to. This experiment includes a human skull! The person it belonged to willed his body to science. Doctors took the skull and put a device that measures radiation inside it. Then they covered the bone with a plastic face. With it, they are able to tell how much space radiation penetrates a live astronaut's skull and reaches the brain. Using this data doctors can design radiation shields to protect astronauts who are in space for long periods of time. Too much radiation could cause sickness or even death.

Another mission specialist and I decide to "borrow" the skull for a minute to have some fun. I get in one of our sleeping bags and pull my head below the opening. The other mission specialist then tapes the skull to the top of the bag so that it looks like the head of whoever is in the bag. The disguise is really scary. The face of the skull has evil-looking eyes, and there are two bolts sticking up from the back of the head that look like horns. Even Captain

Kirk would have run if he had seen this thing floating around his spaceship!

Ever so quietly, my accomplice floats me to the upper deck where the rest of the crew are working. I have my arms through the armholes in the sides of the sleeping bag. Carefully, I push myself to float to the back of an unsuspecting crew member. Hovering behind him, I breathe loudly and slowly, making a deep, raspy, evil sound. The victim turns to investigate and . . . aieeeeeeeeeeeeeeeeeeee! He screams as I grab him! It's the attack of the horned alien from Planet X!

Later, we stuff the sleeping bag with clothes and buckle our alien onto the toilet seat to surprise another crew member. As you can see, astronauts like to joke around, too.

After many hours of conducting experiments, Mission Control tells us that we can go to sleep. Most of the crew tie their sleeping bags downstairs to get away from the sunlight. There are no windows in the lower deck, so we can sleep in the dark. Upstairs, the sun will be rising and setting every forty-five minutes, making it hard to sleep. I want to stay awake awhile longer, so I tie my sleeping bag under the windows that are on top of the aft cockpit. Then I unpack my portable tape player and put on headphones to listen to music. NASA provides the tape player and we are each allowed to bring six music tapes. Some astronauts bring country or rock or easy listening music, but my choice is music by classical composers like Beethoven, Pachelbel, and Bach. I like the slow majesty of their music. To me, it better fits the silent flight of an Earth-orbiting space shuttle and the grand sights passing below.

With these soothing melodies in my ear, I get in my sleeping bag and watch our beautiful world slowly glide by. The shuttle is flying upside down, so the windows on top of the cockpit are facing the earth. It's like being in a hammock with the world in your face.

The other crew members are asleep, and Mission Control is watching the shuttle data to make certain nothing goes wrong. Gravity is holding us in orbit so nobody needs to "steer" the shuttle.

The only sound in the cockpit is the soft whoosh of the fans that cool the electronic equipment. My mind struggles with the strange reality. It's so different from anything I've ever known on Earth. I'm traveling almost five miles each second! At that speed I could fly from Los Angeles to New York in just ten minutes! Yet our motion makes no sound. Always in the past, when I've been traveling fast on a bicycle or in a car or on a train or plane, the faster it went, the louder the noise. Sometimes—like in a fighter airplane, for instance—there was lots of noise. But now, there's no noise. Nothing. No air rushes by the cabin. No engines roar. Nothing!

Adding to the strangeness of the situation is that I'm floating inside my sleeping bag with no force on my body. You don't need a bed or a floor to sleep in weightlessness. The air is your mattress. In fact, the only reason we use bags is so we don't float around and bang into something. You could actually sleep by clipping a tether to your belt loop, hooking it someplace, and just floating on the end

of the line like a kite. Some astronauts have done that.

But I'm in my sleeping bag, listening to Beethoven's violins, floating in an absolute stillness, watching the beautiful Earth. The sight is the very definition of the word *beautiful*.

Many kids ask me if astronauts watch television on the space shuttle. No, we don't. We don't receive ground television. But even if we did, we would never watch it. For entertainment everyone does exactly what I'm doing. They watch Earth. If you were up there, you would do the same thing, too.

I feast my eyes on the glory of Earth. The primary color is blue, for we live on a water planet. What would aliens from a strange desert world who have never seen water think of ours? Would they assume that any intelligent earth life must live in all that "blue stuff"? Would they land their flying saucer in the ocean? Maybe at the bottom of the oceans there are flying saucers with drowned aliens inside.

The clouds thrill me as much as they did when I watched them as a kid. In some places they are scattered across the ocean like little puffs of popcorn. In other places they completely cover the earth. There are great milky swirls of low pressure areas, like the swirls you see going down the bathtub drain. Feathery mare's-tails (cirrus clouds) look like they are painted on the blue sea. Thunderstorms are another joy. Even from my great height, it's obvious they rule the sky. Sometimes there are lines of them, standing shoulder to shoulder like warrior chiefs

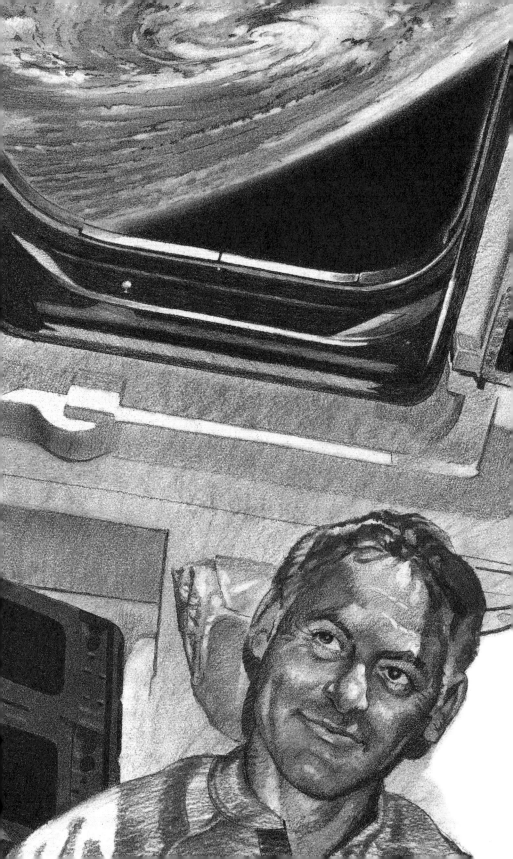

wearing great feathered headdresses. At other times they are just scattered across the ocean. But always their tops are smeared into long, pointed anvils by invisible jet streams.

I turn my attention to the sky. It is absolutely, totally black. And the sun is absolutely, totally white. You can't look directly at the sun, but in your side vision you can see its brilliant white rays. Unlike sunlight seen from Earth, it has no yellow in it.

There's also a quarter-moon looking very lonely in the huge blackness. It doesn't appear any bigger than it does when you see it from Earth. Remember, the moon is 240,000 miles away. We're only three hundred miles closer! That's like being on one side of the classroom looking at a globe on the far side, and then taking a one-inch step toward the globe. It doesn't look any bigger. You can think of an orbiting space shuttle as having taken just a tiny, tiny step toward the moon.

The brightest planets are also visible from the cockpit windows. Even though I'm still on the day side of Earth, I can see Jupiter and Saturn. If Venus were up, I would be able to see it also. But the planets look no different than they look from Earth. They appear as bright stars. They are tens of *millions* of miles away, so being three hundred miles closer doesn't make any difference.

Sirius, the brightest star, is also visible. It's just a steady point of light. There's no twinkle to it as you see on Earth. That's because its light has reached me without going through air. It's the atmosphere that causes stars to twinkle.

But Sirius is the only star I can see. Why? Where are the others? I don't see them because there is too much sunlight reflecting off Earth and the shuttle. That causes the pupils of my eyes to close and cuts off the dim light that is coming from the other stars. They're out there, but I can't see them in daylight. It's just like trying to see stars from the middle of a city. You can't. You have to go into the country away from lights so the pupils of your eyes will open wide and take in the dim starlight. So now you can laugh when you see science-fiction TV programs, like *Star Trek*, showing stars out the windows during daylight.

Silently, *Atlantis* glides eastward and the sun sinks behind it. Below, the tallest thunderstorms cast shadows that are hundreds of miles long. Now comes the most beautiful sight of all. As the sun sets, the earth's atmosphere acts like a prism and splits the light into its individual colors. For a moment, after the sun is completely down, the horizon is outlined with a brilliant rainbow of colors: red, orange, yellow, turquoise, blue, and purple. The colors get dimmer and dimmer as we fly farther and farther to the east. Finally they blink out. Then, there's no trace of the earth. We're swallowed by the black. It's as if we've flown into a deep, deep cave.

I remove my headphones, yawn, and close my eyes. It's time to go to sleep. But it's hard to turn off my brain. I'm worried about tomorrow. The team is depending on me. I will have to use the robot arm to grab our secret payload and lift it from the shuttle's cargo bay. What if I'm not good enough? What if I make a mistake? What if I can't do it? Back in Houston, I practiced a thousand times in a simulator that looked like a video game. I also practiced lifting giant helium balloons out of a simulated shuttle cargo bay with a simulated mechanical arm. The helium made the balloons weightless, as our cargo will be. But practicing with video games and balloons is one thing. Working with a real arm and a real cargo is something else. One mistake, and I could ruin the mission. I feel like the field goal kicker who is warming up on the sidelines of a football game. The team has gotten the ball within range of the goal. They've done all they can do. Time is running out. The kicker will have just one chance to win the game.

I'm like that kicker. The members of my team, the NASA team, have done all they can. They have put me in position. Tomorrow, I'm going to have one chance to win. With that thought comes a nibble of fear. I don't want to let the team down. I don't want to let the nation down. Everyone is counting on me.

But in the end my exhaustion overcomes the worry, and I fall asleep.

I awaken early for the big day and sail headfirst to the lower deck. The rest of the crew are still asleep. What a strange sight that is! Like bats, some of them are on the wall floating upside down in their sleeping bags. One is asleep on the ceiling. And all of them have their arms floating outward from their chests. That's what happens when you fall asleep in weightlessness. Your arms float in front of you. It looks weird, as if the crew is in suspended animation.

It's time to use the bathroom, so I slip behind a curtain and face the monstrosity that is our toilet. Except for the seat, it doesn't look anything like your toilet at home. For one thing, it has no water in it. In weightlessness, water wouldn't flush, so you need something else to carry the waste away. Our toilet uses airflow.

There are several switches and valves on its front, and on each side are things that look like handles. These are really "thigh-holders," bars to twist over your legs to keep you from floating off the toilet seat. You don't want that to happen! Then, there's a long, flexible hose coming up from the front of the toilet. That's the urinal. In the shuttle, liquid and solid waste go into different places. The solid waste goes into an opening on the top of the toilet, while urine goes into the hose. There is even a separate container for toilet paper. You can't put paper down our toilet. And there are several checklists on the bathroom wall to remind you how to operate everything.

After turning on a couple of switches, I urinate into the hose. How do women do that in space? They put a curved piece of plastic on the hose and hold it against their bodies. For men and women, though, the hose works the same way. It's like a vacuum cleaner, and the urine is sucked away. On a trip to Mars, that urine would be recycled into drinking water, but on the space shuttle, we dump our urine overboard. Don't worry, though. That doesn't mean it's raining down on Earth. The sun will dissolve the urine.

Airflow is also used for solid waste collection, but that process is a little more complicated. You sit on the toilet, clamp your legs with the thigh-holders, and open a valve. The valve turns on a ring of air jets that encircle the inside opening of the toilet seat. Those jets shoot air toward your rear end. As it bounces off your body, it carries the waste away from you and into a big tank. After you're done, you close a valve that traps the waste. It isn't dumped in space. It's brought back to Earth.

Suddenly, rock music blares from our speakers. Mission

Control is waking us up. "Good morning, *Atlantis!*"

"Good morning, Houston!" the commander answers the call. It's not really morning where we are. We're over the deserts of Australia, and it's late afternoon. But we ignore earth time when we're in a shuttle. We're spinning around the world every ninety minutes, crossing another time zone every four minutes. It would be crazy to try to set our watches every four minutes! So we ignore earth time and do everything according to a clock that started at liftoff. It's called the MET (Mission Elapsed Time) clock. Right now, that clock says it's morning, so everybody says, "Good morning."

The crew member who was sick yesterday still doesn't feel well and asks for a shot of medicine from our medical kit. Our crew "doctor" prepares a hypodermic needle with an injection that will stop the vomiting. The doctor is really just a Marine astronaut who was given a little medical training back in Houston. This will be the first shot he's ever given! Would you like to get a shot from a Marine? No way!

The injection goes okay, but as the "doctor" withdraws the needle, the patient moves. That tears a tiny hole in his skin, and he starts to bleed. It's nothing serious, but it gives us a chance to watch bleeding in weightlessness. The blood doesn't "run" or drip as it does on Earth. It's weightless, like everything else in the cockpit. So it just bubbles on the skin. It grows bigger and bigger until it's a red marble. I watch one of these spheres come loose and float in the center of the cockpit like a ruby planet. What strange things you see in weightlessness! Finally, we stop the bleeding with a bandage and return to work.

"*Atlantis*, you have a GO to grapple the payload."

The moment has finally arrived. My hands are sweaty with excitement, and I wipe them on my shirt. I slip my feet under the canvas loops on the floor and grab the two joysticks. On my right side is a television screen. A TV camera at the end of the mechanical arm sends pictures to this screen. By looking at those pictures, I can pretend I'm riding on the tip of the arm. The two joysticks allow me to "fly" it wherever I want. It's just like a jet fighter video game at an arcade.

I twist and turn the joysticks and watch from the windows as the arm bends and moves like a human arm. In fact, it's modeled after a human arm. It has a shoulder joint that connects it to the shuttle, an elbow joint that bends just like your elbow, and a wrist joint that moves like your wrist.

On the television, I see the secret satellite come into view. Then, I see the foot-long spike sticking out of it. That's what I'm after. Slowly, I move the joysticks to bring the end of the arm over the spike. In the TV screen, the spike gets bigger and bigger and bigger, until it finally disappears inside a "can" on the end of the arm. I squeeze a joystick trigger, and some cables twist around the spike. The arm is now firmly attached to the satellite.

That was the easy part. Lifting the giant machine without damaging it will be the tough part. There's very little

room. If I bang it into the side of the shuttle, some dangerous things could happen. A fuel tank might be ripped open and cause an explosion. I might damage the shuttle's cargo bay doors so they wouldn't close. If that happened, we couldn't return to Earth. We'd be stranded in orbit, slowly dying as our oxygen was used up. So any mistake could ruin the mission and might even threaten our lives. It's a huge responsibility. I'm scared, but I have confidence in myself and the way the team trained me.

Another mission specialist flips the switches to release the latches that are holding the satellite in the cargo bay. It's finally free to pull upward. Very, very carefully, as if I'm taking apart a bomb, I use the joysticks to bring it higher. I keep looking back and forth from the window to the television screen. My concentration is intense. My heart is pounding. I'm holding my breath. Weightless drops of sweat ooze from my pores and tickle my face. I duck my head into my shirt sleeve to wipe the sweat away.

One foot, two feet, three feet. Higher and higher I bring the machine. Other crew members help me by watching out the window and using other TV cameras.

"Stop!" somebody yells. I release the controls. "You're getting too close to the back wall."

I look at the television and make a correction with the joysticks.

Five feet, six feet. Higher and higher I lift. Ten feet, twelve feet. I start to breathe again. It's finally clear of the space shuttle. I've done it! The monster satellite is floating on the end of the arm, out of danger.

The rest is easy. The commander floats to my side and grabs the joysticks that control the space shuttle. After I release the machine, he will fire the shuttle's maneuvering rockets to move us away from it.

"I'm ready when you are, Mike."

"Let's do it."

I squeeze a trigger, and the cables unwind from around the spike. Then I pull back the arm, and the satellite is free. The shuttle vibrates with rocket firings as the commander flies us away.

Against the black of deep space, the secret satellite is left gleaming in the sun. The red, white, and blue of an American flag proudly shines from its side. It's a wonderful moment in my life. Thousands of hours of training have paid off. I did my part for the team. I kicked the field goal. I've put a satellite in orbit that will help guard our country and keep us free.

That evening I'm relaxed enough to want a big supper.
I float to the kitchen. It's called the *galley*. It's just a small
part of the downstairs shuttle cockpit, right next to the
toilet. In fact, our bathroom, kitchen, gym, bedroom, living room, and experiment laboratory all share the same
tiny area.

I select my supper from a locker: a hamburger patty,
mashed potatoes, mixed vegetables, and strawberries for
dessert. It sounds great, until you realize it's all dehydrat-
ed. The water has been taken out of a lot of our food to
make it more compact and save storage space. Our drinks
are the same way. They're powdered: milk, coffee, cocoa,
tea, orange juice, and so on. We don't carry any soft drinks
because carbonated drinks don't work very well in weightlessness.

Each food item is in a separate dish sealed in plastic.
I put them in the galley's rehydration station, where a

machine adds water. A water-gun needle pierces the plastic, and water squirts into the dish. Using my fingers, I squeeze down on the plastic covering and stir the water into the food. Then I put it in the oven. It's not a microwave. Microwave energy could interfere with the shuttle's electronics. So our oven just has hot air blowing around inside it to heat the food.

When it's ready, I cut the plastic top open with some scissors and eat with a fork and spoon just like I would on Earth. Sometimes the food gets loose and you have to catch it. I've seen astronauts swimming around in weightlessness snapping at loose food like sharks chasing fish.

I've got tea to drink, but it's not in a glass. If I tried to drink from a glass in weightlessness, what would happen? Nothing. If I tilted the glass to my mouth, the tea would stay in the bottom. So we have to drink with straws. We have aluminum pouches with various flavored powders inside. At the rehydration station, we push the water-gun needle into the end of the pouch and add water. After we pull out the needle, we push in a straw and use it to suck out the drink.

"Hey, guys, check it out!" One of the crew has squeezed some orange juice from his drink pouch, and it's floating in midair. In weightlessness, all fluids float as balls. So a perfect sphere of orange juice floats in the middle of the cockpit!

"Let's make a solar system!"

I take peanut M&M candies and place them around the orange juice, like planets around the sun. Mercury is a red

M&M. I use a yellow one for Venus. Earth is green. I continue until I have nine M&Ms floating around our orange juice sun. It looks like a scene from a *Star Trek* movie where strange planets circle around a strange star!

Then I attack my creation, gobbling down the candy planets. Finally, I take a straw, touch it to our "sun," and slurp it away. I've eaten our entire solar system!

Another crew member suggests a game of baseball. The commander pitches peanut M&Ms to a mission specialist who uses a pencil to hit the candy to the rest of us. We chase after "pop flies" with our mouths. The games are a fun way to end a very busy and exhausting day.

Bedtime arrives. Mission Control says good night, and the rest of the crew climb into their sleeping bags. As I did last night, I stay awake at the windows and watch the world spin by.

It's dark now. We're on the midnight side of the earth. I float around the cockpit and turn off all the lights. With no reflections on the windows I can see outside. The view takes my breath away!

The Milky Way looks like its name, like milk. It's a white fog of stars. It seems as if I can see trillions of them! Below me, meteors crash into the atmosphere as shooting stars. They make long streaks of fiery orange and white. Sometimes they explode into pieces when they hit the deep part of the atmosphere.

Lightning illuminates the tops of thunderstorms like sputtering light bulbs. Over the warm parts of the earth, where there are lots of thunderstorms, I can see hundreds of flashes a minute. But can I hear the thunder? No. Sound needs something to move through, like air. The space shuttle orbits in space, which is a vacuum. There is no air, so there can't be any sound. In fact, somebody could set off an atomic bomb right outside the window and I wouldn't hear it. *Atlantis* couldn't be rattled by the shock wave of an outside explosion, either. Shock waves can't travel in a vacuum. The next time you watch *Star Trek*, ask your mom and dad if they think the *Enterprise* crew would get thrown around by a "near-miss" explosion. You'll surprise them by knowing more than the producers of the show. If there's no air, there can be no sound or shock waves or vibrations.

A really special treat comes into view. It's an aurora! You've probably heard of the aurora borealis or the northern lights. At the north pole the earth acts like a giant magnet and sucks electrically charged particles from space towards the ground. As those particles strike the atmosphere, they glow. That causes the northern lights. The same thing happens near the south pole. I'm seeing the southern lights. They're spectacular, like enormous green snakes slithering over the antarctic ice!

We float over Australia, and I see city lights. Cities look like glowing yellow spiders because of the roads that come out from their centers. The city of Sydney, Australia, has some clouds covering it, but the lights are so bright they shine through.

Seeing these lights reminds me of another bet you could win with your parents. Ask, "Is it true the only object built by people that an astronaut can see from space is the Great Wall of China?" Almost all adults believe this. Even the TV quiz program *Jeopardy* gave that as the correct answer to a question. But it's the wrong answer! From orbit you can see such things as city lights, vapor trails of airplanes, large smoke trails from factories, long stretches of straight roads, very large buildings, and airport runways.

What's that? I see something moving! A bright point of light is slowly gliding through space! Could it be a UFO? I grab the binoculars and look, but it's too far away. Then, it starts flashing! Are alien creatures trying to signal me?

It's impossible to know for sure, but I have a hunch what the light is. It's not an alien spaceship. It's just another satellite. There are nearly ten thousand pieces of junk floating around the earth. One of those pieces was probably far enough away that the sun was shining on it. I was seeing sunlight reflecting from a piece of junk. It was probably tumbling, and that's what made it appear to flash. See how your eye can be tricked?

But what about UFOs? Are we alone in the universe? Have other creatures flown to Earth to examine us? There's no way to know for sure. Many people have reported seeing strange things. Some people have even claimed to have been aboard UFOs. But scientists have never found any real proof. What do I believe? Looking from *Atlantis's* windows I see a universe filled with stars. There are so many that it's easy for me to think some have planets circling them. I also think some of those planets might have life. So, I believe there is other life in our universe. But I don't think any creatures in flying saucers have visited us, yet. That's what I believe. What do you believe?

A brilliant rainbow appears on Earth's eastern horizon. Sunrise! Our forty-five minute night is over, and another forty-five minute day is about to start. But the earth below us is still pitch black. It's like being on top of a mountain three hundred miles high. The sun always shines on mountaintops before it shines in valleys. So we have sunlight shining on us in orbit while it's dark on Earth below. Can you think what this means to people who might be watching the sky from the ground? It means they could see us! Just as I saw light reflected from the space junk, they would be looking into a dark sky and *Atlantis* would be reflecting the sunlight! So you can see satellites from Earth. Just go outside about an hour before sunrise or an hour after sunset and stare at the sky. Within a few minutes you will probably see a moving point of light. It won't be an airplane. It won't have any red, green, or flashing lights on it. It will be a satellite!

Atlantis streaks farther eastward, and the sun rises high enough to flood the earth with light. A new day comes to the Pacific Ocean. I see rings of coral islands that look like floating necklaces. On a large island, smoke drifts away from an active volcano. The long white vapor trail of a jet crossing the sea is also visible. It's probably an airliner going from Australia to Los Angeles. It will take those people thirteen hours to get across the Pacific Ocean. *Atlantis* will make the same flight in about thirty minutes!

The Hawaiian Islands come into view. Clouds cover the

tops of the volcanoes like ice cream on a cone. Many more jet vapor trails appear in the sky. Some of them crisscross each other like a giant game of tick-tack-toe.

For a moment I hear the whirr of the toilet fan. The last crew member is getting ready for bed. Then *Atlantis* becomes as still as a sleeping house. I'm very tired, too, and I know I should get some rest, but my brain begs me to stay awake a little while longer.

Far to the east, I see a change. Brown appears on the horizon. It's California. *Atlantis* is approaching the western coast of America. Los Angeles appears as a gray smudge. Smog covers it. Inland, I see snowcapped mountains and huge deserts. Edwards Air Force Base, where we will land in a few days, is easy to see because it's built next to a giant dry lake.

The Colorado River cuts through the desert like a twisting, black vein in the earth's body. I can see the large lakes that it fills: Lake Powell, Lake Mead, and Lake Havasu. Las Vegas, Nevada, glistens in the sun.

A beautiful mixture of red and tan colors passes underneath. It's the Grand Canyon! I'm right over it! The sight makes me think of Nature's patience and power. It took millions of years for water to carve through thousands of feet of earth to make the canyon.

I look south and see a giant hole in the ground. What is it? Then, I remember. It's a meteor crater. Forty-nine thousand years ago a meteor crashed into the earth near present-day Winslow, Arizona, and left the hole. Can you

imagine what that must have been like? A black rock the size of a small house had been tumbling through empty space for billions of years. Maybe, at one time, it had almost collided with another planet in another galaxy. Maybe it had just missed getting sucked into a black hole. Maybe some alien spacecraft had to put up its deflector shields to keep from being hit by it. But on its intergalactic journey it missed everything until it passed too close to our earth. Then, our gravity grabbed it and pulled it down.

There were probably no humans living in North America when it crashed, so the only witnesses would have been prehistoric animals. What would they have seen? Let your imagination take you to that moment. . . .

A plain of amber grasses stretches to a distant, smoking volcano. A small herd of woolly mammoths slowly walks toward a stream. Near them, a saber-toothed tiger eats a bison he recently killed. In the sky, giant condors wheel in circles waiting for the leftovers. It's a clear and quiet summer day in prehistoric Arizona.

The tiger is the first to see the meteor. He glances upward from his meal and watches the strange appearance. The huge object is still fifty miles overhead, but air friction has already heated it to thousands of degrees. It glows brighter than the sun and leaves a long trail of white smoke behind it.

The other animals also begin to notice that something is different. A cluster of bison stare at the meteor while continuing to chew the grass and swish their tails. A mother mammoth senses danger and bellows for her calf to come closer. The tiger also feels uneasy and gives up on his meal. He bounds away toward his cave.

Then the panic starts. The fiery object grows huge. It fills the sky above the animals. There's still no sound because it's traveling at 45,000 miles per hour, many times faster than the speed of sound. But just the brightness is enough to stampede the animals. They run in all directions, stirring up clouds of dust in the process.

But there's no escape. The meteor slams into the earth with an explosive force that is equal to fifteen million tons of dynamite. Everything within miles of the impact is instantly killed. Even far away, animals are killed by the rain of dirt and boulders that the impact throws into the air. Hot pieces of rock fall in forests and start raging fires. The sonic boom of the meteor finally reaches Earth and cracks across the plain, but there's nothing alive to hear it. Where all the animals were is now nothing but a smoking hole four thousand feet wide and six hundred feet deep.

Can you see it? As I glide over the crater, I can see the story as clearly as a movie.

Another river appears. It's the Rio Grande. A dark patch spreads from its eastern shore. It's Albuquerque, New Mexico! It's my home!

The sight chokes me with tears. They flood my eyes and cling in weightless drops to my eyelids. I blot them away, but more follow. I'm not ashamed. I'm not embarrassed. I'm overcome with happiness. From three hundred miles high, I'm watching my dream come true. I want to shout my joy for all the world to hear!

More memories of the dream flash in my mind's eye like photographs from a picture album. One shows me sitting in the cockpit of my dad's plane, pretending to be a pilot. Another captures my balsa wood glider soaring through the crystal-blue New Mexican sky. I can see my airplane coloring books and Tinker-Toy planes and my telescope. I can see myself watching the stars from my front yard, from the very place now passing three hundred miles beneath me! I can see everything about my dream. Everything . . .

RUSSIAN SPUTNIK CIRCLING EARTH!

That was the newspaper headline on October 4, 1957. I was twelve years old.

That night I stood in my front yard. My brothers and sister and parents were with me. Up and down the block, other families were also in their yards. It was like Halloween. Everybody was out. Everybody was talking. Everybody was excited. Some people had brought radios into their yards, and the voices coming from the radios were excited, too. The entire neighborhood, the entire city, in fact people across the entire country were standing outside watching the birth of the space age. The Russian *Sputnik*, the first satellite, was flying over, and we were all outside to watch it.

In Albuquerque it was cold and clear, with the cream of the Milky Way spilling across the sky. Shooting stars occasionally streaked through the black and brought "oooohs" and "ahhhhs" from the crowd.

Then, just as the newspaper had predicted, a tiny light appeared on the southwestern horizon and slowly, silently glided over our heads. Voices were hushed by the sight. People stood in awe. Some cried. Some were frightened. The Russians were our bitter Cold War enemy, and *Sputnik* proved they were better than we were. If they had missiles that could put satellites in orbit, it was feared they could also hurl hydrogen bombs to America. But I was too young to be afraid. I was excited. I wanted to fly where *Sputnik* was flying!

A month later *Sputnik II* carried a dog into orbit. Then, in January 1958, America launched its first satellite. The country was wild with space fever! Everybody was infected: newspeople, politicians, teachers, scientists, moms and dads. Walt Disney produced TV programs about space travel. Songs were written about satellites. The Boy Scouts started a space merit badge. Toy companies started selling model kits of satellites and rockets. Schools had space days. Students went on space field trips to planetariums and museums. "Moon Watch" clubs were formed to observe the new satellites. I joined one of these clubs and spent hundreds of hours staring into space watching Sputniks, Explorers, Vanguards, Echoes, and Telstars. Those were just some of the satellite names.

It was during these exciting days that my imagination was captured by rocketry. I would stay glued to the TV, watching launch after launch. In these early days, many rockets only went a few feet before blowing up in clouds of orange flame. But some worked beautifully, rising into the Florida sky on thunderous columns of fire.

I wanted to know everything about rockets. I went to the library and read about them. I bought books about them. In fact, I still have my favorite childhood rocket book: *The Conquest of Space* by Willy Ley. More than any other book, I loved this one. It did much more than merely explain how rockets work. It had beautiful paintings that showed what it would be like in space and on other planets. At night I would fall asleep reading it and dream of being on the moon or Mars. In the morning I would risk being late for school by trying to read just a few more pages. *The Conquest of Space* taught me the power of books and the power of reading. No television, movie, or video can ever fill the imagination like a book.

Besides reading about rockets and space travel, I also wrote to NASA for information. They sent me photos and fact sheets. I looked at these and then sent them my suggestions on how they could make their rockets better. I even told them they could use my designs for free! I laugh, now, to think I told NASA I had better designs than they did. But I was so caught up in my dream of space flight I really believed I could do anything. I really believed I could design a better rocket than NASA. That's the great part of a dream. Dreams let you believe in yourself. Dreams let you do anything. Dreams let you be anything.

By the age of thirteen, I was a space geek. My classmates were in love with rock stars and cars. They had posters on their bedroom walls of Corvettes and T-Birds, of Elvis

Presley and the Beatles. But on my walls were posters of rockets: Atlases, Jupiters, and Titans. I couldn't tell the difference between a Ford and a Chevy. I didn't know any pop songs. But I could tell you everything about NASA's rockets and satellites.

At this time in my youth there were no toy rockets like the ones you can now buy in hobby stores. If you wanted to experiment, you had to build your own. Rocket clubs were organized for that purpose. Every school had one, and I joined ours. Under the supervision of teachers, rocket designs and rocket fuel formulas were explained. Homemade rockets were soon being built and launched by kids all over the country. There were reports in the newspapers of some of these reaching altitudes of 30,000 feet! Some kids even talked about trying to orbit their own satellites!

Initially, I had adult supervision for my experiments. Then, like many kids, I learned how to get the chemicals to make rocket fuel by myself. I stopped going to the rocket club meetings and started doing my own experiments. Now, I can see how dangerous that was. My rockets got bigger and bigger, until they were taller than I was. Instead of a few ounces of fuel they soon required ten or fifteen pounds of it. I would take them into the desert, light a fuse, and run for cover. Sometimes they blew up and sent steel pieces flying over my head, just like a bomb. Other times they disappeared in the sky, and I never found them again. Only a miracle saved me from serious injury. My dream could have ended in blindness or burns or even death. As it was, many other children were injured, and some were killed, by their rocket experiments. Am I making this up? No. In fact, while I was an astronaut, I met a man who was blind and missing some fingers. He told me that when he was a child, one of his homemade rockets blew up in his face and caused the injuries. Always remember: Never risk your health or life in an experiment of any kind! Injury and death will end your dream!

On April 12, 1961, another headline rocked America: RUSSIANS ORBIT MAN! His name was Yuri Gagarin, and he became the first human to go into space.

America had already selected its first astronauts. They were called the "Mercury Seven" because there were seven of them and they would fly in the Mercury capsule. But none had yet flown in space when Gagarin was launched. America's rockets seemed to blow up every time they were launched, so they were still being tested. Also, they were less powerful than the Russian rockets and couldn't carry much weight into space.

I was fifteen years old then, and because of America's puny rockets I dreamed that I would be the first American in space! That's crazy, isn't it? But I really did dream that NASA would find its Mercury astronauts were too heavy for the rockets to lift, so they would have to pick some skinny kid to go instead. I dreamed they would pick me! I even stopped drinking milkshakes to stay light.

Of course, nobody from NASA ever knocked on my door and said, "Your rocket is ready, Mike." It was still a wonderful dream. You should never be ashamed or afraid to dream of being anything. Dreams do come true.

The older I got, the more determined I became to be a pilot. I washed cars and mowed lawns to make money for flying lessons. After some instruction, at age seventeen I had my first solo airplane flight. It's another memory of my dream that's as clear as a photograph.

When I lined up the plane on the runway, my heart was thumping in my chest like a big drum. I pushed the throttle forward, and the engine roared until the spinning propeller was invisible. Then, I released the brakes and watched the airspeed increase. Twenty knots, thirty, fifty, seventy knots. I gently pulled the yoke backwards, and the ground seemed to fall away from the plane. I was flying! For the first time in my life I was actually flying! I was a pilot! On that day, and many that followed, I flew over the New Mexican deserts and mountains and dreamed of the day I would be a jet fighter pilot doing the same thing.

In 1963, after graduating from high school, I went to West Point, the U.S. Military Academy. West Point is a very strict school that trained me to be a military officer. It also challenged me to be the best that I could be. At first, that was very scary. Nobody had ever done that before. In grade school and high school nobody had really challenged me to do my absolute best. But West Point did. Bellowing seniors would tell me to run up a mountain or swim across a lake holding a rifle in my hands. In class I was given very difficult tests in every subject, every day. Many, many times, I thought, *I can't do this. I'm not good enough. I'm not smart enough. I'm not strong enough.* But I discovered the most amazing thing. I could!

West Point dared me to be my best. It challenged me mentally and physically. At the time, I had no idea how important that was. But for a dream to come true, you have to know how good you are. Most young people never know, because nobody challenges them. Young people say to themselves, "I can't be a doctor or lawyer or teacher or astronaut. I can't go to college. I'm not smart enough." But you are! You really are much smarter and stronger than you think. To find out, dare yourself. Dare yourself to do better. Dare yourself to read more books, learn more words, do more math, do more than your teacher or parents ask of you. Dare yourself to follow a dream!

As my West Point graduation approached, I was very excited. I was going into the Air Force. Soon, I thought, I would be in pilot training. I would learn to fly supersonic jets! The sky wouldn't even be able to hold me. I would take my jet higher and faster than anyone had ever been before. My sonic booms would rattle windows as I climbed and dived all over the sky. Nobody would ever beat me when we practiced dogfighting. I would go to test pilot school and learn to fly the fastest jets, the way Chuck Yeager did. I'd be a top gun. Finally, after many years of training, I would be ready to be an astronaut. What a wonderful, beautiful dream it was. I had my life planned. I knew exactly what I wanted.

Then something terrible happened. A few days before graduation, my commander called me into his office. "Mike," he said. "I have the results of your physical exam for pilot training. You failed the vision test. The doctor says you need eyeglasses."

He didn't have to say anything else. I knew the rules. The Air Force would not let anybody be a pilot without perfect eyesight. I needed glasses, so I could never be a jet fighter pilot. It was the end of the world for me. I went to my room and cried. My dream was over.

Imagine wanting something very, very much. Maybe it's a new bicycle or a baseball glove. Maybe it's a position on the school cheerleading squad or the lead role in the school play. Whatever it is, it's all you can think about. Night and day you dream about having it. Maybe you work very hard to get it. Maybe you spend hours every day shooting baskets or practicing gymnastics to get on a team. You practice and work and study. It seems as if your whole life is at stake. Then, at the last minute, you're told that you can never have it. Maybe you're told that somebody better than you got the position. Maybe you're told you can't be something because of a problem with your health. But, whatever the reason, you're told that your dream is over.

That's what it was like for me when I was told I could not be a pilot. There would be no jet fighters, no test pilot school, no top gun, no astronaut job. It seemed as if somebody had cut out my heart. I cried.

Now, though, I can see the important lesson this experience taught me. I learned you cannot always have what you want. Sometimes things happen that you cannot control. I had no control over my eyesight, so I couldn't be a pilot. I had to find another dream and follow it.

I couldn't be a jet fighter pilot, but I could still fly in jets that had two seats. So that became my new dream. I would be the best fighter "backseater" in the Air Force. I trained to operate the radar and radios and electronic equipment in the rear cockpit of Air Force fighters. It wasn't the "star" position. The pilot had that. But it was still a very important job, and I dared myself to do my best at it.

When I was twenty-five, I went to Vietnam. I had to leave my wife and two babies and go to fight in a terrible war. There, we flew very low and fast over the enemy and took pictures of their airfields and bridges so the bombers could attack them. Red tracers of machine-gun fire and exploding shells streaked by my cockpit. When we flew at night the enemy couldn't see us, but it was even more dangerous. We had to fly in deep valleys at six hundred miles per hour and depend on our instruments and radar to keep from crashing into the mountains.

I was very scared in Vietnam, and I learned another lesson. When I was a little boy, I used to play "war" with my friends and think it would be a lot of fun to shoot guns and drop bombs. But real wars are not fun. They're not like the ones you see in the movies and on TV. Young people get killed in real wars and never return to see their families and children or their mothers and fathers. Many of my West Point classmates were killed or seriously injured. They lost legs and arms or were horribly burned or disfigured.

Something very important in space happened when I was in Vietnam. On July 20, 1969, Neil Armstrong became the first person to walk on the moon! I listened to him say, "That's one small step for a man . . . one giant leap for mankind." I watched the movies of him skipping in the moon dust, and I wanted so badly to be an astronaut. But I knew that dream was dead. NASA would only select people who were test pilots, and I could never be one of those because I wore glasses.

After Vietnam, the Air Force sent me to England for four years. This was during the Cold War, when Russia was our enemy. We trained in our jets in case a real war should start. That never happened, but the training was dangerous and more people died. It was another lesson that wars are very sad.

In 1974 I returned to America and went back to college to become an aeronautical engineer. If I couldn't be a pilot or an astronaut, I could still help to design and test the planes and rockets that the pilots and astronauts would fly. At this school, I once again dared myself to do my best. I graduated with honors.

Next, I went to Edwards Air Force Base in California for another special school that taught me how to test airplanes. You would love to go to this school! Imagine getting in the back seat of a supersonic jet and taking measurements while the pilot flies it as fast as it can go. It was awesome! And because of another self-dare, I again graduated from this school with honors.

One day, as I was getting out of my jet, a friend rushed up to tell me some incredible news. NASA had just announced they were going to select new astronauts for their latest rocket, the space shuttle. Some of these astronauts would be called *mission specialists*. They would do experiments and space walks and release satellites. What was so incredible about this? Mission specialists didn't have to be pilots! They could wear glasses! Imagine my joy at this news! Ten years earlier I had been told I could *never* be an astronaut because of my eyesight. Now, the dream was back! I had a chance!

But was I good enough to be an astronaut? Weren't astronauts like supermen? When they were kids, didn't they all get straight-A's in school and graduate number one in their college classes? Weren't they the smartest and bravest people on Earth? The newspapers and magazines said they were.

I knew I wasn't the smartest or bravest person on Earth. I didn't get straight-A's on my report cards. And I had been scared many times when I was flying. But I had always dared myself to do my best. Now, because of those dares, I had a very good record to mail to NASA.

But just think what *could* have happened. I could have given up ten years earlier. Remember? I had been curled on my bed, crying, thinking my life was over. I could have quit daring myself. For ten years, I could have done just enough to squeak by. But if I had, I would have lost this one chance to be an astronaut. You can never go wrong by doing your best.

I had a chance, but it seemed a very slim one. NASA was expecting over ten thousand applications for only thirty-five astronaut positions! How could I possibly be picked? There were just too many people.

Many months later I was amazed to be called to NASA for an interview. I sat at the end of a long table, and astronauts who had walked on the moon asked me questions. Did they ask me about math and science and aeronautical engineering? Did they ask me to name all the planets or explain how a rocket works? No. They wanted to know about me as a person. They wanted to know about my dream!

"Mr. Mullane," they said, "tell us about your childhood. How long have you wanted to be an astronaut?"

I told them the story of my dream, of wanting to be a pilot, of building rockets.

They also wanted to know if I could get along with other people. NASA is a giant team made up of men and women of all races and religions. NASA wanted men and women who could be part of a team.

The interview lasted two hours. Next, I was sent to doctors for a physical examination. NASA will only pick people as astronauts who are in good physical condition. Since I had never used tobacco or drugs or abused alcohol, my lungs and heart and the rest of my body were in perfect shape.

I went home to wait for NASA to call with a decision. It was November 1977. Would I be selected as an astronaut? Would my dream come true? One week went by without a call. Two weeks. A month. It was torture.

The Air Force moved me to Idaho and I waited for the

call there. December passed, and I was sure that NASA had not picked me.

Then, one cold January morning the phone rang. It was NASA. I had been selected as one of the first mission specialist astronauts!

I cheered! I screamed my head off! I skipped around the room! It was like hitting a home run to win the World Series! It was like catching a touchdown pass in the Super Bowl! It was wonderful! Incredible! I WAS GOING TO BE AN ASTRONAUT!

That night I walked into the Idaho desert and looked at the sky. It was cold and bright with stars. Satellites drifted silently over my head as dim specks of light. *Someday soon*, I thought, *I will be up there with them.*

It's our third morning in space, and Mission Control wakes us with more rock music. Everyone feels great. The one crew member who had been vomiting is now completely well. One of the crew floats me a foil pouch of coffee, and I sip it while watching the giant satellite I released yesterday. It's many miles away, but the reflecting sunlight has turned it into a morning star brighter than Venus.

Yes, it's a great day.

Then a call comes from Mission Control that changes our mood.

"*Atlantis*? Houston. We were wondering if you saw anything break off the top of the right booster during ascent?"

The commander grabs the microphone. "Negative, Houston. Ascent looked nominal. What's up?"

"In a review of the ground films of your launch, engineers thought they saw something come off the tip of the booster."

I get a sinking feeling in my stomach. If something broke off, it could have hit the belly of the shuttle. The belly is covered with thousands of very fragile heat tiles. They are made out of silica, the same stuff that's in sand, and they could be destroyed by an impact. That doesn't affect us while we're in space. But on reentry, the friction of the atmosphere could turn *Atlantis* and everything in it into ash. The heat tiles are the only things that keep us from burning up.

But what can we do? How can we look at the belly of the shuttle to find out if it's damaged? The NASA team has the answer.

"*Atlantis*, we want Mike to use the robot arm to look at the belly. We're transmitting some instructions on how to do that."

Once again the team is depending on me. But now I'll be doing something that I haven't practiced. They want me to bend the robot arm around the side of the shuttle and look underneath. The TV camera on the end of the arm will transmit pictures of what the belly looks like.

I'll have to be extra careful. The arm will be bent at a crazy angle. It will be very close to the shuttle. One mistake and I could damage the tiles for sure.

As I grab the joysticks and begin the maneuver, I'm scared at the thought of what I might see. Suppose there is a lot of damage? There's no way we could repair it. There's no way to space walk to the belly of the shuttle, and even if we could, we wouldn't have any tools to make such a repair.

I shiver with fear as I imagine what would happen to *Atlantis* if there is major damage. On reentry, fire would melt a hole in the belly and then start burning through wires and equipment. Alarms would sound in the cockpit as hydraulic pumps, electrical generators, computers, and other equipment began to fail. The fire alarm would go off as the heat started a fire in the cockpit. The other mission specialists and I would leave our seats to fight the blaze. But the reentry g-forces would make me weigh three-hundred and sixty pounds. My legs would buckle, and I would crash to the floor and have to crawl to the fire. Air would start leaking out, and a shrieking hiss would be added to all the other alarms. To keep us alive, our pressure suits would automatically inflate, making the arms and legs as hard as an inflated tire. We would be like the Tin Man in *The Wizard of Oz*, barely able to move.

Meanwhile, the commander and pilot would be doing everything possible to keep the shuttle flying straight. They would be madly flipping through checklists and shouting emergency procedures to each other. But in the end, atmospheric friction would win the battle. The shuttle would start groaning and vibrating as pieces of the wings burned off. The last hydraulic pump would explode, and the shuttle would slowly spin out of control. From the ground it would look like a giant shooting star, scattering flaming pieces of aluminum across the sky. I would be dead.

That's what I'm thinking as I carefully twist the robot arm under the fuselage.

Finally, the belly heat tiles come into view on the television screen. We gasp. Hundreds of tiles are scraped and gouged! At least one tile is completely missing. What's going to happen to us on reentry?

"*Atlantis*, this is Mission Control. You have a GO for the deorbit burn."

"Roger, Houston. Go for the burn. We're coming home."

For the past two days, Mission Control has reviewed the TV images of the belly. They think *Atlantis* will survive reentry. They can't be certain, but they believe the damage to most of the tiles is minor. Even the missing tile should be no problem since the shuttle was designed to withstand reentry with a few gaps in the tiles.

But the TV image from the robot arm camera was not very good, and we couldn't see the entire belly. What if there are huge areas of missing tile that were hidden from the camera?

Five . . . four . . . three . . . two . . . one . . . BOOM!

The OMS engines fire. *Atlantis* is pointing backwards in orbit, so the engines are now slowing us down. The shuttle is doing the same thing that you do when you try to stop yourself on a water slide or a snowy sled ride. You use your hands and feet to try and push yourself back up the hill. Usually you don't stop. You just slow down a little. When a shuttle comes out of orbit, it does the same thing. Its OMS engines try to thrust it backwards. That doesn't stop the shuttle, but it slows it down enough so its orbit altitude decreases. It decreases enough so that *Atlantis* falls into the atmosphere. Atmospheric friction then slows it down for landing.

After about two minutes, the engines shut down and the commander turns *Atlantis* around and pulls the nose up. We want the belly to hit the atmosphere first.

From this point on, *Atlantis* is a glider. For the next hour it will slowly fall earthward toward the dry-lake runway of Edwards Air Force Base. It will glide across the Indian Ocean, Australia, and the Pacific Ocean. It will glide for 12,000 miles! The OMS engines can't be used in the atmosphere, so there's no way to fly around and look for a runway. If there's an error in our computer navigation, we could fall too fast and crash into the Pacific Ocean. Or, we could come in too slowly. Then we would be too high to land at Edwards, and we would crash in the deserts of Arizona or New Mexico. We must rely on *Atlantis*'s computers to steer us correctly.

For the first half of reentry, it's very quiet in the cockpit. We don't have much to do except watch the instruments, the way we did during launch. Out the windows I see nothing but black. We're on the night side of the earth.

The instruments show us getting steadily closer to

California. Our altitude meter shows a slow descent. We're gliding at almost 18,000 miles per hour, but we don't hear noise or feel vibrations. The earth's air doesn't really get thick enough to affect the shuttle until about fifty miles from the ground. Since we started at three hundred miles, we fall in silence for about two hundred fifty miles.

I see something falling from the ceiling. It's an M&M candy! We must have lost it playing M&M baseball. While we were in orbit, things floated everywhere. The M&M I'm watching must have floated into a corner. Now, as we pass through the top of the atmosphere, the shuttle is slowing down. Everything in the cockpit that isn't put away slowly falls toward the floor. We're no longer weightless. The falling M&M is an indication that we are experiencing the very beginning of reentry g-forces. Other "lost" things begin to experience the same force. A piece of plastic, a small screwdriver, a tiny battery, and a bit of granola bar all join the M&M in a slow drift to the floor. It's "raining" lost garbage.

The g-forces also affect my body. My arms feel heavy. It's hard to hold up my head. Even the small g-forces feel huge because my body is used to being weightless.

We fall farther and farther. The atmosphere gets thicker and thicker. The g-forces slowly increase to one-quarter the force of gravity . . . one half . . . then normal gravity. My body is at its usual weight, but it seems to weigh a ton. I'm crushed into my seat.

When I see the fire, fear makes me forget about the invisible elephant on my shoulders. It's still night outside, but the windows are now covered with an orange glow. The shuttle has struck the thick atmosphere, and friction is heating its belly to thousands of degrees. The glow is the hot air. Or is it? Maybe it's the shuttle's aluminum skin melting. Maybe the tile damage is so severe that we're burning up like a shooting star. Everybody stares at the instruments. If we were melting, the instruments would show various emergencies. So far, though, everything is nominal.

The orange glow brightens. It turns pink and then white hot. Brilliant flashes come through the upper windows. The super-hot air is flowing around the shuttle and forming a wake behind us, like the one behind a boat. It flashes through the top windows like lightning. I try to look up through those windows. If the shuttle is burning, I'll see flaming pieces of it flying off. But the g-forces have paralyzed me in my seat. I can't move enough to see from the windows. All I can do is watch the instruments and pray that the tiles are holding up.

The sun rises in our faces and reveals the Pacific Ocean. Through the fire on the window, I can see a lace of clouds covering it. It's a beautiful day.

We enter radio blackout. The air surrounding *Atlantis* is now so hot that it blocks all radio signals. Mission Control is blind. They have no data to see what's going on. *This is it*, I think. This is the hottest the shuttle will get. In some places it's three thousand degrees! I'm sitting in the middle of a fireball. The windows are white with the heat. If we can only get through this, we'll be safe. A call from

Mission Control will mean the blackout is over and the damaged tiles have protected us.

The seconds on the clock seem to drag. Ten, eleven, twelve, thirteen. Fear fills the cockpit. Will we make it? Will the tiles hold out?

Twenty-one, twenty-two, twenty-three seconds.

The commander's hand hovers over the control stick. If something goes wrong, he's ready to take control from *Atlantis's* computers.

Thirty-eight, thirty-nine, forty, forty-one seconds.

My eyes are like pinballs. They bounce from instrument to instrument. The navigation display shows a flashing green "bug"—the shuttle—moving precisely along the planned trajectory. Meters, dials, and flickering numbers show everything is nominal.

Forty-seven, forty-eight, forty-nine, fifty seconds.

What's keeping Mission Control?

A "bump" ripples through the cockpit. My heart leaps into my throat. The commander's hand jerks closer to the control stick. What was it? Did something finally burn off the shuttle? All eyes sweep across the instruments. But everything is still okay. We decide it must have been a tiny change in the density of the upper atmosphere.

The seconds seem to move like hours.

Then . . .

"*Atlantis*, Houston is back with you. Your energy and ground track look nominal."

"Roger, Houston. We read you loud and clear."

I can almost hear everybody sigh. We're breathing again. We're through the worst heat and still alive! We're going to make it!

Now the vibrations begin. We're passing thirty miles altitude, and the air is really thick. At least it feels thick to a huge glider that's traveling through it at ten thousand miles per hour! It howls around the cockpit and shakes us like a roller coaster. It's also rapidly slowing us down and putting us in danger.

Danger? What danger?

We're in danger of fainting. The same g-force that pulled the loose M&M to the floor is now pulling blood from our heads. I get tunnel vision. There's not enough blood reaching the part of the brain that allows me to see. My side vision slowly gets blacker and blacker until I feel like I'm looking through a tunnel. I'm in danger of complete blackout, of fainting.

I have a way to fight the g's. Underneath my pressure suit, I'm wearing an anti-g suit. It's a rubber bladder that goes around my stomach and legs. I twist a control knob on the leg of my suit, and air rushes into the bladder. It squeezes my stomach and legs very hard. My belly button feels like it's being crushed into my backbone, the squeeze is so tight. It hurts. But I don't care. The terrible squeeze of the suit cuts down the blood flow to my legs and allows my heart to send it to my brain. It's keeping me from fainting. But the stomach squeeze makes it difficult to talk. We grunt like weight lifters.

The shuttle continues to fall, gliding closer and closer to the earth.

Land ho! The coast of California comes into view. Los Angeles sparkles in hazy sunlight. In a minute, the city will be hit with our shock wave. It will rattle windows with a BOOM-BOOM. Edwards Air Force Base appears. There isn't a cloud in the sky. It's perfect landing weather.

Things begin to happen quickly now. The shuttle is plunging earthward with all the grace of a brick. The commander will have only one chance for a landing. To help him, a steady stream of information comes from Mission Control. The radios are filled with a babble of technical talk.

"TACANs look good."

"Roger."

"Air data probes are out."

"Roger, incorporate air data."

"Good MLS lock."

"I'm going CSS."

"Winds are two-five-zero at five knots."

"Energy is nominal."

"I'm on the HAC."

The desert grows bigger and bigger in the windows. *Atlantis* is in a diving turn for the runway.

"Radar altimeter is in . . . three hundred knots . . . looking good . . . four thousand feet . . . two hundred ninety knots . . . three thousand . . . two thousand . . . pre-flare."

The commander raises *Atlantis's* nose. We're only a minute from landing, and the wheels are still up. Why do we wait so long? It's because *Atlantis* is a glider. If we lower the wheels early, the extra air-drag confuses the computers. So we wait until the last second. Many people worry about this and say, "But what happens if the wheels don't come down?" It doesn't matter if the wheels don't come down at fifty thousand feet or one thousand feet. We'll still crash-land. You can't keep a glider in the air to try some type of emergency wheel lowering. So, you might as well wait until the last second and let the shuttle fly for as long as possible as a streamlined glider.

"Gear!" The commander finally orders the wheels to be lowered. The pilot presses two buttons and the landing gear begins to unfold.

"Three hundred feet . . . two hundred . . . one hundred . . . two hundred five knots . . . fifty feet . . . two hundred two knots . . . "

The pilot keeps up a steady call of our altitude and airspeed so the commander can concentrate on the runway.

"Twenty feet . . . ten . . . five . . . touchdown." The shuttle shakes and rattles over the dry lake desert. The nose comes down in a puff of dust.

We're safely on the ground. The mission is over. In the cockpit we all cheer and shake hands. But my heart is a little sad. I wish I could still be in space, living my dream. What a glorious, wonderful, magnificent dream it's been!

But it's somebody else's turn now. Somewhere a girl or boy is watching on TV as *Atlantis* rolls to a stop. Model airplanes and rockets and *Star Trek* posters decorate this dreamer's bedroom. Books about rockets and astronauts fill the bookshelves.

Is it you? Do you have the dream of being an astronaut? Or do you dream of being a teacher, lawyer, doctor, nurse, scientist, engineer, or anything else? How do you make that dream come true? Or do dreams only come true for a few very smart, special kids?

I wasn't particularly smart. I had to work very hard to get good grades. In high school I was a B+ student. And I certainly wasn't special. I didn't come from a famous family. We weren't rich, and we weren't poor. I had four brothers and a sister. I was the second child. When I was nine years old, my father caught polio, and he lived the rest of his life in a wheelchair. Except for that, my family was an ordinary one.

So my dream didn't come true because I was different from all the other boys and girls my age. I played with trucks and frogs. I played Little League baseball. I was in the Cub Scouts and the Boy Scouts. Sometimes I got in trouble at school or with my parents and was punished for it. One time I was even arrested by the police for throwing a water balloon at some other teenagers. There was nothing special about me.

Why, then, did my dream of being an astronaut come true? How can you turn a dream into reality?

First, you must believe in yourself. You must believe that you can be anything, do anything. Remember . . . dare yourself! There's another boy or girl inside you who wants to prove how smart he or she really is. Give that part of you a chance. Offer yourself a dare. Dare yourself to dream BIG! Dare yourself to believe you can be anything!

Does that mean it will automatically happen? Just because you believe you can be a doctor or nurse or teacher or scientist or astronaut, will it happen? No. Just believing won't make a dream come true. Michael Jordan would never have become a great basketball player by just sitting around dreaming about it. He worked very hard to develop the tools needed to be a star. He worked to develop his endurance and speed and agility. People always need tools to turn their dreams into reality. What tools do you need?

You need an education. Without an education dreams shrivel up and die. You can wish all you want. You can believe in yourself. But without an education, you will never see your dream come true. Stay in school! Study!

What's the most important subject to study? That's an

easy one. Reading. If you can't read, your education stops. You can't study math, history, science, or anything else. You must be a good reader for a dream to come true!

What else do you need?

You need your health. You can have everything I've talked about. You can believe in yourself. You can be a straight-A student. You can be the best reader in the world. But if you have damaged your health with drugs, alcohol, or tobacco, will your dream come true? No. These are poisons that will take your dream and your life. Take care of your body. It's the only one you'll ever have, and you're the only person who can guard it from danger.

Respect for others is another key to making dreams come true. You can't dream of being a pilot and hate to work with people of the opposite sex. The person who will guard your tail in a dogfight may be a woman. You can't be an astronaut and hate people whose backgrounds differ from yours, or who have a different skin color. Your commander, the person who holds your life in his or her hands, could be black, white, Asian, Hispanic, in other words, anyone.

For a dream to come true, you must be a team player. You must respect everybody regardless of gender or race or religion. Remember my astronaut interview? Did NASA ask me to do a calculus problem? No. They wanted to know if I could work well with other people. They wanted to know if I was a team player. Are you? Could you be on a team with somebody who is a different color or believes in a religion different from yours?

In your dream quest, you must also be prepared to face things that you cannot control. Remember my story. I had believed in myself. I had worked hard in school. I had taken care of my body and learned to respect other people. But I had no control over my eyesight. When that weakened, my dream of being a fighter pilot and test pilot and top gun and astronaut came to a screeching stop. But if something you cannot control interferes with your dream, what do you do? Do you give up? Or do you dare yourself to follow another dream? That's what I did. I dared myself to be the best backseater in Air Force fighters. I dared myself to be the best aeronautical engineer. I didn't know it at the time, but those dares kept my dream of being an astronaut alive for ten years! Don't ever give up. When things you can't control get in the way, then dare yourself into another dream. Who knows, maybe the second or third dream will make the first one come true. It did for me.

Atlantis is stopped now. A convoy of support trucks is speeding toward us. In the upper cockpit we follow checklists to power down the shuttle. We unbuckle our safety belts, climb down the ladder to the lower cockpit, and duck through the hatch. Stairs have been driven up to the side of the shuttle. For a moment, we all stand on the top platform breathing deeply of the wonderful scent of desert sagebrush. The commander, pilot, and other mission specialists file down the stairs. I follow them, holding on to the rail in case my wobbly legs should collapse. When a TV

camera momentarily focuses on me, I smile and wave. Though they don't know it, I'm waving at all the dreamers who are watching. I'm waving at the kids who someday will feel the roar of mighty engines at their backs and the crush of g-forces on their chests and see the black of space racing into their faces.

AUTHOR'S NOTES

What did we find when we looked at *Atlantis*'s belly? More than seven hundred heat tiles had been damaged so badly that they would later have to be replaced. Only one tile was completely missing, but the others around it had kept *Atlantis*'s aluminum skin from melting. We had been very lucky.

What had caused all this damage? In the factory, the very tip of the right-side rocket booster had been made too weak. The wind pressure during launch had broken it off, and it had hit the belly. To make certain it would not happen on another mission, NASA changed the way the boosters were built to make them stronger.

On Being an Astronaut

There are two types of NASA astronauts: pilot astronauts and mission specialist astronauts. Pilot astronauts sit in the front seats and have the controls and instruments to fly the shuttle during launch and landing. The pilot astronaut who sits in the front left seat is also called the **commander**. He or she is the overall boss. The pilot astronaut who sits in the front right seat is called the **pilot** and helps the commander fly the spaceship. He or she is really like a copilot in a regular airplane. **Mission specialists** are the crew members (usually three) who do most of the work once the shuttle reaches orbit. They operate the robot arm, do experiments, go on space walks, and release satellites.

What kind of an education do you need if you want to be an astronaut? NASA requires all astronauts to have a college degree in math, science, or engineering. You can't be an astronaut if you get a degree in English, history, music, law, or other non-science fields. NASA says you only need a bachelor's degree to be eligible for an astronaut job, but almost everybody chosen so far has at least a master's degree. Ask your teacher to explain bachelor, master's, and doctorate degrees.

Do you have to be a pilot or be in the military to be an astronaut? No. About one-third of the astronauts are civilians who are not pilots. But if you're not a pilot you can only apply to be a mission specialist astronaut.

To be a pilot astronaut, NASA requires that you have at least one thousand hours of jet flying time. For this reason all pilot astronauts are military flyers. You should plan on being a military test pilot if you want to be a pilot astronaut.

The Space Transportation System (STS)

The mission of the space shuttle, or STS as NASA calls it, is to carry satellites and experiments into orbits about one hundred fifty to three hundred fifty miles above the earth. While it can't fly to the moon (that's about 240,000 miles away), the shuttle can do something no rocket before it could ever do. It can be recycled. Before the shuttle, all of our rockets, including the moon rockets, were "throwaway" rockets. In other words, during their missions all of their parts were jettisoned to fall into the water or burn up in the atmosphere. The only thing that ever came back was the capsule with the astronauts in it. Even the capsule was never used again. It was sent to a museum. But almost all of the STS can be reused, which saves money.

There are three parts to the STS:

The *orbiter* is the winged vehicle that carries the astronauts. Six orbiters have been built: *Enterprise, Columbia, Challenger, Discovery, Atlantis*, and *Endeavour*. The orbiter *Challenger* was destroyed and its astronauts were killed on January 28, 1986, when a hole burned through the side of one of the solid-fueled rocket boosters.

The **external tank** (ET) is the giant orange fuel tank that is attached to the belly of the orbiter. The ET is the only part of the STS that is not reused. It is jettisoned into the atmosphere.

The **solid-fueled rocket boosters** (SRBs) are the giant white booster rockets that are attached to each side of the ET. When they burn out, they are jettisoned and parachute into the ocean. Tugboats pick them up and tow them to shore so they can be cleaned, refilled with solid fuel, and used over again.

The Future

The shuttle is not the end of America's space program. It's just a step, like the Mercury, Gemini, Apollo, and Skylab space projects before it. Soon, if our Congress gives NASA the money, the next step will be taken. We will work with the Russians, Japanese, Canadians, and Europeans to assemble a space station in orbit about three hundred miles above Earth. We need such a station so astronauts can live and work in space for very long periods. While the shuttle may be recyclable, it can only stay in orbit for about two weeks before it runs out of electricity. That's not enough time to complete many experiments. If we could stay in orbit for years on a space station, we might be able to make new medicines, metals, computer chips, and many other things that will help us have better lives on Earth.

After the space station, NASA plans to return to the moon. Astronauts would build a permanent moon base with telescopes and other instruments to help us better understand our universe.

Then, NASA wants to send people to the planet Mars. Who will be the first human to set foot on the red planet? Could it be you? A mission to Mars could begin in as little as thirty years. The astronauts who take that trip will be about forty to forty-five years old. That means they are now students between ten and fifteen years old. That's your age! That means YOU could be the first Martian! Imagine that incredible journey. . . .

After blasting away from earth orbit at a speed of twenty-five thousand miles per hour, you would begin a long silent drift into deep space. Earth would shrink to a ball and then to a marble, and finally it would appear as just a bright star. You and your crew members, men and women from several nations, would now depend on each other more than ever.

Then, as the months passed, Mars would grow bigger and bigger. Its polar ice caps and two small moons, Deimos and Phobos, would become visible. Olympus Mons, a volcano three times taller than the tallest mountain on Earth, would appear. You would see the great Valles Marineris, a canyon so long and so deep it makes our Grand Canyon look puny.

Finally, with the red planet looking huge in your window, you would fire your braking rockets. The first firing would stabilize you in Martian orbit. A second firing, weeks later, would start you to the surface. Clouds of reddish dust would swirl around your windows and block your view, but your instruments would help guide you. A warning light and a thump would indicate landing. You would open the hatch and back down the ladder. For a moment you would hesitate, trying to control your excitement. Slowly you would open your hands and let the weak Martian gravity pull you the last few inches to the ground. Then, you would raise your boot. Through tears of joy, you would look at the first human footprint on another planet . . . *your* footprint.